LIFE
Lessons
WITH MAX LUCADO

BOOK OF ROMANS
GOD'S BIG PICTURE

MAX LUCADO

Prepared by
THE LIVINGSTONE CORPORATION

THOMAS NELSON
Since 1798

NASHVILLE DALLAS MEXICO CITY RIO DE JANEIRO

LIFE Lessons

WITH MAX LUCADO

CONTENTS

HOW TO
STUDY THE BIBLE

This is a peculiar book you are holding. Words crafted in another language. Deeds done in a distant era. Events recorded in a far-off land. Counsel offered to a foreign people. This is a peculiar book.

It's surprising that anyone reads it. It's too old. Some of its writings date back five thousand years. It's too bizarre. The book speaks of incredible floods, fires, earthquakes, and people with supernatural abilities. It's too radical. The Bible calls for undying devotion to a carpenter who called himself God's Son.

Logic says this book shouldn't survive. Too old, too bizarre, too radical.

The Bible has been banned, burned, scoffed, and ridiculed. Scholars have mocked it as foolish. Kings have branded it as illegal. A thousand times over the grave has been dug and the dirge has begun, but somehow the Bible never stays in the grave. Not only has it survived; it has thrived. It is the single most popular book in all of history. It has been the best-selling book in the world for years!

There is no way on earth to explain it. Which perhaps is the only explanation. The answer? The Bible's durability is not found on earth; it is found in heaven. For the millions who have tested its claims and claimed its promises, there is but one answer: the Bible is God's book and God's voice.

As you read it, you would be wise to give some thought to two questions. What is the purpose of the Bible? and How do I study the Bible? Time spent reflecting on these two issues will greatly enhance your Bible study.

What is the purpose of the Bible?

Let the Bible itself answer that question.

Since you were a child you have known the Holy Scriptures which are able to make you wise. And that wisdom leads to salvation through faith in Christ Jesus. (2 Tim. 3:15 NCV)

The purpose of the Bible? Salvation. God's highest passion is to get his children home. His book, the Bible, describes his plan of salvation. The purpose of the Bible is to proclaim God's plan and passion to save his children.

That is the reason this book has endured through the centuries. It dares to tackle the toughest questions about life: Where do I go after I die? Is there a God? What do I do with my fears? The Bible offers answers to these crucial questions. It is the treasure map that leads us to God's highest treasure--eternal life.

But how do we use the Bible? Countless copies of Scripture sit unread on bookshelves and nightstands simply because people don't know how to read it. What can we do to make the Bible real in our lives?

The clearest answer is found in the words of Jesus. He promised:

Ask, and God will give to you. Search, and you will find. Knock, and the door will open for you. (Matt. 7:7 NCV)

The first step in understanding the Bible is asking God to help us. We should read prayerfully. If anyone understands God's Word, it is because of God and not the reader.

But the Helper will teach you everything and will cause you to remember all that I told you. The Helper is the Holy Spirit whom the Father will send in my name. (John 14:26 NCV)

Before reading the Bible, pray. Invite God to speak to you. Don't go to Scripture looking for your idea; go searching for his.

Not only should we read the Bible prayerfully; we should read it carefully. *Search and you will find* is the pledge. The Bible is not a newspaper to be skimmed but rather a mine to be quarried.

Search for it like silver, and hunt for it like hidden treasure. Then you will understand respect for the LORD, and you will find that you know God. (Prov. 2:4–5 NCV)

Any worthy find requires effort. The Bible is no exception. To understand the Bible you don't have to be brilliant, but you must be willing to roll up your sleeves and search.

Be a worker who is not ashamed and who uses the true teaching in the right way. (2 Tim. 2:15 NCV)

Here's a practical point. Study the Bible a bit at a time. Hunger is not satisfied by eating twenty-one meals in one sitting once a week. The body needs a steady diet to remain strong. So does the soul. When God sent food to his people in the wilderness, he didn't provide loaves already made. Instead, he sent them manna in the shape of *"thin flakes like frost . . . on the desert ground"* (Ex. 16:14 NCV).

God gave manna in limited portions. God sends spiritual food the same way. He opens the heavens with just enough nutrients for today's hunger. He provides *"a command here, a command there. A rule here, a rule there. A little lesson here, a little lesson there"* (Isa. 28:10 NCV).

Don't be discouraged if your reading reaps a small harvest. Some days a lesser portion is all that is needed. What is important is to search every day for that day's message. A steady diet of God's Word over a lifetime builds a healthy soul and mind.

A little girl returned from her first day at school. Her mom asked, "Did you learn anything?"

"Apparently not enough," the girl responded, "I have to go back tomorrow and the next day and the next . . ."

Such is the case with learning. And such is the case with Bible study. Understanding comes little by little over a lifetime.

There is a third step in understanding the Bible. After the asking and seeking comes the knocking. After you ask and search, then knock.

Knock, and the door will open for you. (Matt. 7:7 NCV)

To knock is to stand at God's door. To make yourself available. To climb the steps, cross the porch, stand at the doorway, and volunteer. Knocking goes beyond the realm of thinking and into the realm of acting.

To knock is to ask, What can I do? How can I obey? Where can I go?

It's one thing to know what to do. It's another to do it. But for those who do it, those who choose to obey, a special reward awaits them.

The truly happy are those who carefully study God's perfect law that makes people free, and they continue to study it. They do not forget what they heard, but they obey what God's teaching says. Those who do this will be made happy. (James 1:25 NCV)

What a promise. Happiness comes to those who do what they read! It's the same with medicine. If you only read the label but ignore the pills, it won't help. It's the same with food. If you only read the recipe but never cook, you won't be fed. And it's the same with the Bible. If you only read the words but never obey, you'll never know the joy God has promised.

Ask. Search. Knock. Simple, isn't it? Why don't you give it a try? If you do, you'll see why you are holding the most remarkable book in history.

INTRODUCTION TO THE BOOK OF ROMANS

At the moment I don't feel too smart. I just got off the wrong plane that took me to the wrong city and left me at the wrong airport. I went east instead of west and ended up in Houston instead of Denver.

It didn't look like the wrong plane, but it was. I walked through the wrong gate, dozed off on the wrong flight, and ended up in the wrong place.

Paul says we've all done the same thing. Not with airplanes and airports, but with our lives and God. He tells the Roman readers:

There is no one who always does what is right, not even one. (3:10 NCV)

All have sinned and are not good enough for God's glory. (3:23 NCV)

We are all on the wrong plane, he says. All of us. Gentile and Jew. Every person has taken the wrong turn. And we need help.

In this profound epistle, Paul explores all the wrong options and takes us to the only correct one. The wrong solutions are pleasure and pride (chapters 1 and 2); the correct solution is Christ Jesus (3:21–26). According to Paul, we are saved by grace (undeserved, unearned favor), through faith (complete trust) in Jesus and his work.

The letter concludes with practical instruction for a growing church, including thoughts on spiritual gifts (12:3–8), genuine love (12:9–21), and good citizenship (13:1–14). The final chapters provide brilliant instruction for dealing with everything from church division to difficult brethren.

Romans is a life-changing letter for people who are willing to admit they are sinners. For those who admit they are on the wrong plane, the letter provides the correct itinerary.

Read it and take note. That flight home is one you don't want to miss.

LESSON ONE

RIGHT
WITH GOD

MAX
LUCADO

REFLECTION

The book of Romans offers an expanded and detailed look at God's special plan for the human race. It will show you the "before and after" conditions of your life in relation to Jesus Christ. As you begin this study, consider your lifestyle before you became a Christian. Identify some of the major changes Christ has made in your life.

SITUATION

The apostle Paul wrote this letter to the group of Christians in Rome, the capital of the Roman Empire. He composed this letter of Christian doctrine after years of missionary work. Though he had not yet visited Rome, he thought highly of the believers there. He wanted to spend time with them as he had done with so many other fledgling churches around the Mediterranean Sea. This letter is Paul's way of saying, "Here are all the central lessons I would teach you if I could spend time with you." In this passage, Paul describes the glory and power of the gospel of Christ.

OBSERVATION

Read Romans 1:16–32 in the NCV or the NKJV.

NCV

¹⁶I am proud of the Good News, because it is the power God uses to save everyone who believes—to save the Jews first, and also to save those who are not Jews. ¹⁷The Good News shows how God makes people right with himself—that it begins and ends with faith. As the Scripture says, "But those who are right with God will live by trusting in him."

¹⁸God's anger is shown from heaven against all the evil and wrong things people do. By their own evil lives they hide the truth. ¹⁹God shows his anger because some knowledge of him has been made clear to them. Yes, God has shown himself to them. ²⁰There are things about him that people cannot see—his eternal power and all the things that make him God. But since the beginning of the world those things have been easy to understand by what God has made. So people have no excuse for the bad things they do. ²¹They knew God, but they did not give glory to God or thank him. Their thinking became useless. Their foolish minds were filled with darkness. ²²They said they were wise, but they became fools. ²³They traded the glory of God who lives forever for the worship of idols made to look like earthly people, birds, animals, and snakes.

²⁴Because they did these things, God left them and let them go their sinful way, wanting only to do evil. As a result, they became full of sexual sin, using their bodies wrongly with each other. ²⁵They traded the truth of God for a lie. They worshiped and served what had been created instead of the God who created those things, who should be praised forever. Amen.

²⁶Because people did those things, God left them and let them do the shameful things they wanted to do. Women stopped having natural sex and started having sex with other women. ²⁷In the same way, men stopped having natural sex and began wanting each other. Men did shameful things with other men, and in their bodies they received the punishment for those wrongs.

²⁸People did not think it was important to have a true knowledge of God. So God left them and allowed them to have their own worthless thinking and to do things they should not do. ²⁹They are filled with every kind of sin, evil, selfishness, and hatred. They are full of jealousy, murder, fighting, lying, and thinking the worst about each other. They gossip ³⁰and say evil things about each other. They hate God. They are rude and conceited and brag about themselves. They invent ways of doing evil. They do not obey their parents. ³¹They are foolish, they do not keep their promises, and they show no kindness or mercy to others. ³²They know God's law says that those who live like this should die. But they themselves not only continue to do these evil things, they applaud others who do them.

NKJV

16For I am not ashamed of the gospel of Christ, for it is the power of God to salvation for every-one who believes, for the Jew first and also for the Greek. 17For in it the righteousness of God is revealed from faith to faith; as it is written, "The just shall live by faith."

18For the wrath of God is revealed from heaven against all ungodliness and unrighteousness of men, who suppress the truth in unrighteousness, 19because what may be known of God is manifest in them, for God has shown it to them. 20For since the creation of the world His invisible attributes are clearly seen, being understood by the things that are made, even His eternal power and Godhead, so that they are without excuse, 21because, although they knew God, they did not glorify Him as God, nor were thankful, but became futile in their thoughts, and their foolish hearts were darkened. 22Professing to be wise, they became fools, 23and changed the glory of the incorruptible God into an image made like corruptible man—and birds and four-footed animals and creeping things.

24Therefore God also gave them up to uncleanness, in the lusts of their hearts, to dishonor their bodies among themselves, 25who exchanged the truth of God for the lie, and worshiped and served the creature rather than the Creator, who is blessed forever. Amen.

26For this reason God gave them up to vile passions. For even their women exchanged the natural use for what is against nature. 27Likewise also the men, leaving the natural use of the woman, burned in their lust for one another, men with men committing what is shameful, and receiving in themselves the penalty of their error which was due.

28And even as they did not like to retain God in their knowledge, God gave them over to a debased mind, to do those things which are not fitting; 29being filled with all unrighteous-ness, sexual immorality, wickedness, covetousness, maliciousness; full of envy, murder, strife, deceit, evil-mindedness; they are whisperers, 30backbiters, haters of God, violent, proud, boast-ers, inventors of evil things, disobedient to parents, 31undiscerning, untrustworthy, unloving, unforgiving, unmerciful; 32who, knowing the righteous judgment of God, that those who prac-tice such things are deserving of death, not only do the same but also approve of those who practice them.

EXPLORATION

I. In what different ways does God reveal himself to people? (For a few biblical illustrations, see Psalm 19:1, 8; John 12:49; 14:10, 26; Acts 14:17; Romans 1:16, 20; I Corinthians 2:13; I John 5:13.)

2. How have some people provoked God to anger?

3. How and why is the truth of the gospel hidden from some people?

4. What happens when God lets people go their own way?

5. How does this passage describe a way we can find freedom from the bondage of sin?

INSPIRATION

Behind him, a trail of tracks.

Beneath him, a pounding stallion.

Before him, miles of trail to cover.

Within him, a flint-rock resolve.

Squinty eyed. Firm jawed. Rawboned. Pony Express riders had one assignment—deliver the message safely and quickly. They seized every advantage: the shortest route, the fastest horse, the lightest saddle. Even the lightest lunchbox.

Only the sturdy were hired. Could they handle the horses? The heat? Could they outrun robbers and outlast blizzards? The young and the orphans were preferred. Those selected were given $125 a month (a good salary in 1860), a Colt revolver, a lightweight rifle, a bright red shirt, blue trousers, and eight hours to cover eighty miles, six days a week. Hard work and high pay. But the message was worth it.

The apostle Paul would have loved the Pony Express. For he, like the riders, had been entrusted with a message.

"I have a duty to all people," Paul told the Roman church (Rom. 1:14 NCV). He had something for them—a message. He'd been entrusted as a Pony Express courier with a divine message, the gospel. Nothing mattered more to Paul than the gospel. "I am not ashamed of the gospel," he wrote next, "because it is the power of God for the salvation of everyone who believes" (Rom. 1:16 NIV).

Paul existed to deliver the message. How people remembered him was secondary. (Else why would he introduce himself as a slave? Rom. 1:1). How people remembered Christ was primary. Paul's message was not about himself. His message was all about Christ. (From *It's Not About Me* by Max Lucado)

REACTION

6. How would you describe righteousness to a new believer?

7. Based on this passage, explain what is required to be right with God. What does John 14:6 say?

8. How have you seen the righteousness of Christ transform a person's life? Explain.

9. In what areas of your life do your sinful desires tend to interfere with living a righteous life?

10. How does this passage encourage you to live by faith?

LIFE LESSONS

Whether we are new in our faith or have trusted in Christ for many years, all of us struggle with the challenge of keeping our faith immediate—up to the moment. Our human tendency is to fall back on our righteousness, our track record, our ability to do and be good rather than placing our hope in Christ. Really understanding that Jesus wants our complete trust is an ongoing process, a one-day-at-a-time reality. Yesterday's challenges to faith may inform today's responses, but they don't exempt us from living by faith today. If you are considering Christ, putting faith in him is an unavoidable starting point, but that decision isn't the end of it. Each day is a fresh opportunity to acknowledge and experience living by Christ's righteousness, not ours. If you recently trusted Christ, what lessons in living by faith have you already learned? If you've been a believer for a long time, what disciplines have you learned about keeping faith lively, or have you been "spiritually coasting" for a while?

DEVOTION

Father, forgive us for being witnesses of your majesty and yet living as though you do not exist. Forgive us, Father, when we sometimes put more hope in the things of this earth than in the incredible promises of your heaven. Have mercy on our hardened hearts. Transform us into your likeness.

For more Bible passages on righteousness, see 1 Samuel 26:23; 1 Kings 10:9; Habakkuk 2:4; Zephaniah 2:3; Malachi 4:2; Romans 3:21; 8:10; Galatians 3:11; and 2 Timothy 3:16.

To complete the book of Romans during this twelve-part study, read Romans 1:1–32.

JOURNALING

Write out a prayer of thanks to God for saving you from a life of sin and bringing you into a right relationship with him.

LESSON TWO

KNOWING
CHRIST

MAX
LUCADO

REFLECTION

In the last lesson, we traced a long journey that humans have taken away from God. In the beginning humans deliberately rebelled, and now every new generation experiences the results of that rebellion. Repentance is the first step that begins the journey home. The gospel offers hope for the journey. What steps have you taken recently to deepen your relationship with Christ?

SITUATION

Paul was aware that his audience had a divided worldview: Jewish and Gentile. He needed to get the attention of two kinds of thinking. In this chapter he addresses the self-confident Jewish mind that assumed a special place in God's plan, as well as the Gentile mind that was proudly self-reliant. Both ways of thinking needed to undergo a change of perspective, by seeing the human condition from God's holy perspective.

OBSERVATION

Read Romans 2:1–16 in the NCV or the NKJV.

NCV

¹If you think you can judge others, you are wrong. When you judge them, you are really judging yourself guilty, because you do the same things they do. ²God judges those who do wrong things, and we know that his judging is right. ³You judge those who do wrong, but you do wrong yourselves. Do you think you will be able to escape the judgment of God? ⁴He has been very kind and patient, waiting for you to change, but you think nothing of his kindness. Perhaps you do not understand that God is kind to you so you will change your hearts and lives. ⁵But you are stubborn and refuse to change, so you are making your own punishment even greater on the day he shows his anger. On that day everyone will see God's right judgments. ⁶God will reward or punish every person for what that person has done.

7Some people, by always continuing to do good, live for God's glory, for honor, and for life that has no end. God will give them life forever. 8But other people are selfish. They refuse to follow truth and, instead, follow evil. God will give them his punishment and anger. 9He will give trouble and suffering to everyone who does evil—to the Jews first and also to those who are not Jews. 10But he will give glory, honor, and peace to everyone who does good—to the Jews first and also to those who are not Jews. 11For God judges all people in the same way.

12People who do not have the law and who are sinners will be lost, although they do not have the law. And, in the same way, those who have the law and are sinners will be judged by the law. 13Hearing the law does not make people right with God. It is those who obey the law who will be right with him. 14(Those who are not Jews do not have the law, but when they freely do what the law commands, they are the law for themselves. This is true even though they do not have the law. 15They show that in their hearts they know what is right and wrong, just as the law commands. And they show this by their consciences. Sometimes their thoughts tell them they did wrong, and sometimes their thoughts tell them they did right.) 16All these things will happen on the day when God, through Christ Jesus, will judge people's secret thoughts. The Good News that I preach says this.

NKJV

1Therefore you are inexcusable, O man, whoever you are who judge, for in whatever you judge another you condemn yourself; for you who judge practice the same things. 2But we know that the judgment of God is according to truth against those who practice such things. 3And do you think this, O man, you who judge those practicing such things, and doing the same, that you will escape the judgment of God? 4Or do you despise the riches of His goodness, forbearance, and longsuffering, not knowing that the goodness of God leads you to repentance? 5But in accordance with your hardness and your impenitent heart you are treasuring up for yourself wrath in the day of wrath and revelation of the righteous judgment of God, 6who "will render to each one according to his deeds": 7eternal life to those who by patient continuance in doing good seek for glory, honor, and immortality; 8but to those who are self-seeking and do not obey the truth, but obey unrighteousness—indignation and wrath, 9tribulation and anguish, on every soul of man who does evil, of the Jew first and also of the Greek; 10but glory, honor, and peace to everyone who works what is good, to the Jew first and also to the Greek. 11For there is no partiality with God.

12For as many as have sinned without law will also perish without law, and as many as have sinned in the law will be judged by the law 13(for not the hearers of the law are just in the sight of God, but the doers of the law will be justified; 14for when Gentiles, who do not have the law, by nature do the things in the law, these, although not having the law, are a law to themselves, 15who show the work of the law written in their hearts, their conscience also bearing witness, and between themselves their thoughts accusing or else excusing them) 16in the day when God will judge the secrets of men by Jesus Christ, according to my gospel.

EXPLORATION

1. What reason did Paul give for advising the Romans to avoid judging others?

2. Why do people tend to take God's kindness for granted?

3. According to this passage, what guidelines will God use to reward or punish people?

4. If hearing the law does not make people right with God, then what does?

5. How can we tell right from wrong?

INSPIRATION

I've wondered, at times, what kind of man this Judas was. What he looked like, how he acted, who his friends were . . . But for all the things we don't know about Judas, there is one thing we know for sure: he had no relationship with the Master. He had seen Jesus, but he did not know him. He had heard Jesus, but he did not understand him. He had religion, but no relationship.

As Satan worked his way around the table in the Upper Room, he needed a special kind of man to betray our Lord. He needed a man who had seen Jesus, but did not know him. He needed a man who knew the actions of Jesus, but had missed out on the mission of Jesus. Judas was this man. He knew the empire but had never known the Man.

We learn this timeless lesson from the betrayer. Satan's best tools of destruction are not from outside the church, they are from within the church. A church will never die from the immorality in Hollywood or the corruption in Washington. But it will die from corrosion within—from those who bear the name of Jesus but have never met him, and from those who have religion, but no relationship.

Judas bore the cloak of religion, but he never knew the heart of Christ. Let's make it our goal to know him . . . deeply. (From *Shaped by God* by Max Lucado)

REACTION

6. What similarities do you see between Judas and the people Paul addressed in this letter?

7. How does Paul explain the difference between being religious and being right with God? How do we live the difference?

8. What is hypocrisy and why is it harmful to the church? (Jesus' teaching on the subject is recorded in Matthew 6:2–8; 7:1–6; 15:5–9; 23:1–36; and Luke 6:41–42; 12:1–2.)

9. What examples of spiritual corrosion do you see in the church today?

10. In what subtle ways does Satan try to corrode your relationship with Christ?

11. How can you guard against Satan's attacks?

LIFE LESSONS

One area of relentless temptation we can expect to encounter involves our tendency to compare ourselves with others. This type of judging has only one purpose: to make ourselves feel better, superior, and spiritually safe. The Bible consistently points out the dangers and sin of such comparisons. In this passage Paul has shown us that comparisons simply deny the truth that we all stand before a holy God as fallen creatures in desperate need of his mercy. When we forget to include ourselves in that picture, we can't see others clearly.

DEVOTION

Father, we have all failed you in some way. We have taken wrong paths and made wrong choices. We know your law, yet we choose to ignore it. We strive to impress others with our knowledge of you when our hearts are far from you. Forgive us, Father. Guide us into a truer, deeper relationship with you.

For more Bible passages on developing a relationship with Christ, see Matthew 12:50; John 1:12; 15:5; Romans 8:15–17; 2 Corinthians 5:17; Philippians 3:8.

To complete the book of Romans during this twelve-part study, read Romans 2:1–3:8.

JOURNALING

What can I do to deepen my relationship with Christ? How can I know him better?

LESSON THREE

A PRICELESS
GIFT

MAX
LUCADO

REFLECTION

It's easy for us to question God's dealings with us. God's ways are not our ways, and we will never fully understand the mysteries of his justice and holiness and power. What would you do with stubborn humanity if you were God? As the holy Creator, how would you respond to your sinful creatures? Think about how God has worked in your heart and life recently. What about your salvation is still a mystery to you?

SITUATION

Paul has created a stalemate regarding the Law. God's laws are good, he says, but they are incapable of motivating us to live up to God's righteous expectations. Whether the law is present or not, we can't obey it perfectly, so we are still sinners. Quite a predicament! But Paul is only laying the foundation for the good news that will follow here in Romans 3. Here are helpful definitions for three significant theological terms used in Romans: (1) *Justification* refers to God's declaration that we are not guilty for our sins. (2) *Redemption* means that Jesus paid the penalty for our sins by dying on the cross. (3) *Atonement* refers to Christ's sacrifice on our behalf.

OBSERVATION

Read Romans 3:21–31 in the NCV or the NKJV.

NCV

²¹But God has a way to make people right with him without the law, and he has now shown us that way which the law and the prophets told us about. ²²God makes people right with himself through their faith in Jesus Christ. This is true for all who believe in Christ, because all people are the same: ²³All have sinned and are not good enough for God's glory, ²⁴and all need to be made right with God by his grace, which is a free gift. They need to be made free from sin through Jesus Christ. ²⁵God gave him as a way to forgive sin through faith in the blood of Jesus' death. This showed that God always does what is right and fair, as in the past when he was patient and did not punish people for their sins. ²⁶And God gave Jesus to show today that he does what is right. God did this so he could judge rightly and so he could make right any person who has faith in Jesus.

²⁷So do we have a reason to brag about ourselves? No! And why not? It is the way of faith that stops all bragging, not the way of trying to obey the law. ²⁸A person is made right with God through faith, not through obeying the law. ²⁹Is God only the God of the Jews? Is he not also the God of those who are not Jews? ³⁰Of course he is, because there is only one God. He will make Jews right with him by their faith, and he will also make those who are not Jews right with him through their faith. ³¹So do we destroy the law by following the way of faith? No! Faith causes us to be what the law truly wants.

NKJV

²¹But now the righteousness of God apart from the law is revealed, being witnessed by the Law and the Prophets, ²²even the righteousness of God, through faith in Jesus Christ, to all and on all who believe. For there is no difference; ²³for all have sinned and fall short of the glory of God, ²⁴being justified freely by His grace through the redemption that is in Christ Jesus, ²⁵whom God set forth as a propitiation by His blood, through faith, to demonstrate His righteousness, because in His forbearance God had passed over the sins that were previously committed, ²⁶to demonstrate at the present time His righteousness, that He might be just and the justifier of the one who has faith in Jesus.

²⁷Where is boasting then? It is excluded. By what law? Of works? No, but by the law of faith. ²⁸Therefore we conclude that a man is justified by faith apart from the deeds of the law. ²⁹Or is He the God of the Jews only? Is He not also the God of the Gentiles? Yes, of the Gentiles also, ³⁰since there is one God who will justify the circumcised by faith and the uncircumcised through faith. ³¹Do we then make void the law through faith? Certainly not! On the contrary, we establish the law.

EXPLORATION

1. In what ways are all people alike? What do we all share in common, particularly when it comes to God?

2. How can people be made right with God? (It may be helpful to refer to 3:22–24 and Isaiah 52:13–53:12.)

3. Using this passage as an illustration, how does God's plan demonstrate his fairness toward humanity?

4. What should prevent believers from bragging?

INSPIRATION

"Love," Paul says, "never fails" (I Cor. 13:8 NIV). The verb Paul uses for the word *fail* is used elsewhere to describe the demise of a flower as it falls to the ground, withers, and decays. It carries the meaning of death and abolishment. God's love, says the apostle, will never fall to the ground, wither, and decay. By its nature, it is permanent. It is never abolished . . .

Governments will fail, but God's love will last. Crowns are temporary, but love is eternal. Your money will run out, but his love never will.

"How could God have a love like this? No one has unfailing love. No person can love with perfection." You're right. No person can. But God is not a person. Unlike our love, his never fails. His love is immensely different from ours.

Our love depends on the receiver of the love. Let a thousand people pass before us, and we will not feel the same about each. Our love will be regulated by their appearance, by their personalities. Even when we find a few people we like, our feelings will fluctuate. How they treat us will affect how we love them. The receiver regulates our love.

Not so with the love of God. We have no thermostatic impact on his love for us. The love of God is born from within him, not from what he finds in us. His love is uncaused and spontaneous. As Charles Wesley said, "He hath loved us. He hath loved us. Because he would love."

Does he love us because of our goodness? Because of our kindness? Because of our great faith? No, he loves us because of *his* goodness, kindness, and great faith. John says it like this: *"This is love; not that we loved God, but that he loved us"* (1 John 4:10 NIV).

Doesn't this thought comfort you? God's love does not hinge on yours. The abundance of your love does not increase his. The lack of your love does not diminish his. You goodness does not enhance his love, not does your weakness dilute it . . . God loves you simply because he has chosen to do so. (From *A Love Worth Giving* by Max Lucado)

REACTION

5. When did you first realize that salvation is a free gift provided by Christ?

6. What or who helped you reach that realization?

7. In what different ways do people try to earn salvation?

8. Why is it important to understand that salvation is a free gift from God? Why wouldn't that news thrill certain people?

9. Describe how your life would be different without Jesus.

10. How do we receive God's approval?

LIFE LESSONS

What is priceless can't be bought or earned. Eternal life is just such a treasure. We receive it free or not at all. We could never afford it. We could never deserve it. It's God's gift to us, or we don't have it. But it would be a huge mistake to conclude in this case that what is free is cheap. It cost God a great deal, including his Son's life, to provide this gift for us. There's no room for bragging in our response; only gratitude.

DEVOTION

Holy God and Father in heaven, we come to you, aware that we do not deserve to be in your presence. We thank you that you have provided a path for us through the blood of your precious Son. Your saving grace is a priceless gift. Keep us amazed and mesmerized by what you have done for us.

For more Bible passages on the gift of salvation, see John 3:16; Acts 4:12; Ephesians 2:8; 1 Thessalonians 5:9; 1 Timothy 1:15; Titus 2:11; Hebrews 5:7–9.

To complete the book of Romans during this twelve-part study, read Romans 3:9–31.

JOURNALING

How can I tell others about God's free gift?

LESSON FOUR

THE FAITH
OF ABRAHAM

MAX
LUCADO

REFLECTION

To benefit the most from this lesson, take a few minutes to review Abraham's life in the Bible. Here are some key passages: Genesis 12:1–4; 15:1–6; 22:1–18; and Galatians 3:6–9. As you consider Abraham's life, try to think of someone who has been an example of great faith to you. What are the evidences of that person's faith?

SITUATION

In order to make his case for God's ancient plan of salvation, Paul traced the Jewish lineage back to its beginning with Abraham. The original patriarch of the Jewish nation was not himself a Jew. Paul argued that if God granted salvation (righteousness by faith) to Abraham, long before he fathered the Jewish nation, would it not make sense to conclude that God has a plan for the rest of Gentiles? And God's plan has always been based on faith, not lineage.

OBSERVATION

Read Romans 4:13–25 in the NCV or the NKJV.

NCV

¹³*Abraham and his descendants received the promise that they would get the whole world. He did not receive that promise through the law, but through being right with God by his faith.* ¹⁴*If people could receive what God promised by following the law, then faith is worthless. And God's promise to Abraham is worthless,* ¹⁵*because the law can only bring God's anger. But if there is no law, there is nothing to disobey.*

¹⁶*So people receive God's promise by having faith. This happens so the promise can be a free gift. Then all of Abraham's children can have that promise. It is not only for those who live under the law of Moses but for anyone who lives with faith like that of Abraham, who is the father of us all.* ¹⁷*As it is written in the Scriptures: "I am making you a father of many nations." This is true before God, the God Abraham believed, the God who gives life to the dead and who creates something out of nothing.*

¹⁸*There was no hope that Abraham would have children. But Abraham believed God and continued hoping, and so he became the father of many nations. As God told him, "Your descendants also will be too many to count."* ¹⁹*Abraham was almost a hundred years old, much past the age for having children, and Sarah could not have children. Abraham thought about all this, but his faith in God did not become weak.* ²⁰*He never doubted that God would keep his promise, and he never stopped believing. He grew stronger in his faith and gave praise to God.* ²¹*Abraham felt sure that God was able to do what he had promised.* ²²*So, "God accepted Abraham's faith, and that faith made him right with God."* ²³*Those words ("God accepted Abraham's faith") were written not only for Abraham* ²⁴*but also for us. God will accept us also because we believe in the One who raised Jesus our Lord from the dead.* ²⁵*Jesus was given to die for our sins, and he was raised from the dead to make us right with God.*

NKJV

13For the promise that he would be the heir of the world was not to Abraham or to his seed through the law, but through the righteousness of faith. 14For if those who are of the law are heirs, faith is made void and the promise made of no effect, 15because the law brings about wrath; for where there is no law there is no transgression.

16Therefore it is of faith that it might be according to grace, so that the promise might be sure to all the seed, not only to those who are of the law, but also to those who are of the faith of Abraham, who is the father of us all 17(as it is written, "I have made you a father of many nations") in the presence of Him whom he believed—God, who gives life to the dead and calls those things which do not exist as though they did; 18who, contrary to hope, in hope believed, so that he became the father of many nations, according to what was spoken, "So shall your descendants be." 19And not being weak in faith, he did not consider his own body, already dead (since he was about a hundred years old), and the deadness of Sarah's womb. 20He did not waver at the promise of God through unbelief, but was strengthened in faith, giving glory to God, 21and being fully convinced that what He had promised He was also able to perform. 22And therefore "it was accounted to him for righteousness."

23Now it was not written for his sake alone that it was imputed to him, 24but also for us. It shall be imputed to us who believe in Him who raised up Jesus our Lord from the dead, 25who was delivered up because of our offenses, and was raised because of our justification.

EXPLORATION

1. Tell how Abraham became right with God. Abraham's life may have been filled with love for God, good works, and obedience to religious rules. But none of these things made Abraham acceptable to God. What did?

2. How did Abraham receive God's promise? How can others receive it?

3. What obstacles did Abraham overcome to believe God's promise?

4. What does it mean to have a strong faith? Does strength of faith rely on its source or on its object?

5. What words were written for both Abraham and us?

INSPIRATION

Henry Drummond [writes:] "You will find, if you think for a moment, that the people who influence you are people who believe in you. In an atmosphere of suspicion men shrivel up; but in that atmosphere they expand and find encouragement and educative fellowship. It is a wonderful thing that here and there in this hard uncharitable world there should still be left a few rare souls who think no evil. This is the great unworldliness. Love sees the bright side, puts the best construction on every action. What a delightful state of mind to live in! What a stimulus and benediction even to meet with it for a day! To be trusted is to be saved. And if we try to influence or elevate others, we shall soon see that success is in proportion to their belief of our belief in them. For the respect of another is the first restoration of the self-respect a man has lost; our ideal of what he is becomes to him the hope and pattern of what he may become."

This faith moves mountains of inertia in other people. It pulverizes prejudices and impossibilities. This faith is the fruit of God's Gracious Spirit that sweetens a sour world. It replaces suspicion and distrust with friendship and hope and good cheer. It makes our friends, family, and casual acquaintances stand tall.

Faith of this caliber comes from God. If we lack it we must ask for it. He urges us to come boldly requesting good gifts from Him (Luke 11:9–13). He does bestow His Gracious Spirit on those who request His presence and are prepared to cooperate wholeheartedly with His commands (Acts 5:32). He will not withhold any good thing from those who seek His faith in sincerity. He is faithful. (From *A Gardener Looks at the Fruits of the Spirit* by Philip Keller)

REACTION

6. How does Abraham's example inspire you to a deeper faith?

7. How can our life of faith influence others?

8. Describe a time when someone else's faith made a difference in your life.

9. What things can keep our faith from growing?

10. What do you usually do when you experience doubts?

11. What can we learn from Abraham about dealing with hindrances to faith?

LIFE LESSONS

Almost everyone in Abraham's day, as in our own day, had faith of one kind or another. Some of them believed in idols, others believed in luck or fate, and many simply had faith in themselves. Abraham's faith had a divine object. He had faith in God, and he acted on it. The faith people witness in our lives may not automatically communicate the object of our faith. They will see the effects of our faith. If they ask, we must be ready to tell them our faith rests in Jesus Christ. We live by faith because we live in him.

DEVOTION

Father, you accepted Abraham's faith, and you accept ours today. We do not deserve your forgiveness and mercy, yet you give it freely. Thank you for covering our guilt in the blood of your only Son. Continue to strengthen our faith in you, for your glory.

For more Bible passages on faith, see Genesis 15:6; 2 Chronicles 20:20; Isaiah 7:9; Habakkuk 2:4; Matthew 9:29; Acts 15:9; Romans 5:1; 10:17.

To complete the book of Romans during this twelve-part study, read Romans 4:1–5:21.

JOURNALING

How are the people around me impacted by my faith in God?

LESSON FIVE

VICTORY
OVER SIN

MAX
LUCADO

REFLECTION

Habits. The best ones seem impossible to develop; the worst ones show up effortlessly in our lives. Good habits disappear in a heartbeat; bad ones hang on like a painful disability. Think of a time when you conquered a bad habit. How did you do it? Describe how this made you feel.

SITUATION

Paul knows that the human tendency to abuse God's grace runs deep. He returns to the question that began this sixth chapter. Does the reality of God's grace make it possible for us to sin at will without concern about consequences? Absolutely not. Unless we deliberately place ourselves in God's hands, becoming slaves of righteousness, the freedom offered to us in Christ degenerates into slavery of a different kind. Why would we choose to serve the world, the flesh, or the devil, when we have the opportunity to serve our Creator?

OBSERVATION

Read Romans 6:15–23 in the NCV or the NKJV.

NCV

¹⁵*So what should we do? Should we sin because we are under grace and not under law? No!*
¹⁶*Surely you know that when you give yourselves like slaves to obey someone, then you are really slaves of that person. The person you obey is your master. You can follow sin, which brings spiritual death, or you can obey God, which makes you right with him.* ¹⁷*In the past you were slaves to sin—sin controlled you. But thank God, you fully obeyed the things that you were taught.* ¹⁸*You were made free from sin, and now you are slaves to goodness.* ¹⁹*I use this example because this is hard for you to understand. In the past you offered the parts of your body to be slaves to sin and evil; you lived only for evil. In the same way now you must give yourselves to be slaves of goodness. Then you will live only for God.*

²⁰*In the past you were slaves to sin, and goodness did not control you.* ²¹*You did evil things, and now you are ashamed of them. Those things only bring death.* ²²*But now you are free from sin and have become slaves of God. This brings you a life that is only for God, and this gives you life forever.* ²³*When people sin, they earn what sin pays—death. But God gives us a free gift—life forever in Christ Jesus our Lord.*

NKJV

¹⁵*What then? Shall we sin because we are not under law but under grace? Certainly not!*
¹⁶*Do you not know that to whom you present yourselves slaves to obey, you are that one's slaves whom you obey, whether of sin leading to death, or of obedience leading to righteousness?* ¹⁷*But God be thanked that though you were slaves of sin, yet you obeyed from the heart that form of doctrine to which you were delivered.* ¹⁸*And having been set free from sin, you became slaves of righteousness.* ¹⁹*I speak in human terms because of the weakness of your flesh. For just as you presented your members as slaves of uncleanness, and of lawlessness leading to more lawlessness, so now present your members as slaves of righteousness for holiness.*

²⁰*For when you were slaves of sin, you were free in regard to righteousness.* ²¹*What fruit did you have then in the things of which you are now ashamed? For the end of those things is death.* ²²*But now having been set free from sin, and having become slaves of God, you have your fruit to holiness, and the end, everlasting life.* ²³*For the wages of sin is death, but the gift of God is eternal life in Christ Jesus our Lord.*

EXPLORATION

1. Why should Christians avoid sinning?

2. What are some of the consequences of sin? (For added suggestions see the following passages: Ezra 9:6–7; Psalm 66:18; Proverbs 23:29–35; Isaiah 1:4–7; 59:2; Hosea 5:5–7; and Matthew 13:15.)

3. What are the results of obeying God? (The results of obedience to God are described in passages like Exodus 19:5–6; Deuteronomy 5:29; Proverbs 23:17–18; Matthew 12:50; John 14:23; James 1:25; and 1 John 3:22–24.)

4. What example did Paul use to help the Romans understand his point?

5. What does it mean to be a slave of God?

INSPIRATION

Imagine being thrown in jail on suspicion of a charge, left there, virtually forgotten, while the system, ever so slowly caught up with you. You get sick. You're treated harshly. Abused. Assaulted. Would you begin to entertain that feeling of lostness and hopelessness?

Back to the question: "How shall we who died to sin still live in it?" Who would volunteer to be dumped in a jail for another series of months, having been there and suffered the consequences of such a setting? His point: Then why would emancipated slaves who have been freed from sin and shame return to live under that same domination any longer? . . . We have been programmed to think, I know I am going to sin, to fail . . . to fall short today. Since this is true I need to be ready to find cleansing. You have not been programmed to yield yourself unto God as those who have power over sin.

How much better to begin each day thinking victory, not defeat; to awake to grace, not shame; to encounter each temptation with thoughts like, "Jesus, You are my Lord and Savior. I am your child—liberated and depending on Your power. Therefore, Christ, this is Your day, to be lived for Your glory. Work through my eyes, my mouth, and through my thoughts and actions to carry out Your victory. And, Lord, do that all day long." (From *The Grace Awakening* by Charles Swindoll)

REACTION

6. Why do you think people choose to be slaves to sin?

7. Why do believers continue to struggle with sin? (For biblical details regarding temptation, see Matthew 26:41; 1 Corinthians 10:13; Galatians 6:1; and Hebrews 2:17–18; 4:14–16.)

8. What are the benefits of being slaves of righteousness?

9. Why do we let sin control areas of our lives?

10. What can a believer do to break free from sin?

11. How does this passage challenge your attitude toward sin in your life?

LIFE LESSONS

Before we trust in Christ's power and presence in our lives, sin and sinful habits exercise power over us. Our efforts to control them are largely ineffective. Whether or not we fight, we're in a losing battle. Sin controls us. But when we accept Christ, the rules change. Sin and sinful habits no longer have power, though they relentlessly seek to maintain influence over us and to gain our permission to continue their work. Paul tells us that before we knew Christ, we were slaves to sin. But Christ has purchased us and given us our freedom. We can now by the power of Christ say no to sin and experience the power of overcoming sin and sinful habits.

DEVOTION

Father, we know we can live new lives free from the bondage of sin because of the death and resurrection of your Son. You have won the victory over sin and death. Father, we ask you to be the master of our lives. Protect us from the evil one and the temptations of this world. We invite the purifying power of your Holy Spirit to cleanse our lives. May we stay blameless until the day of your return.

For more Bible passages on victory over sin, see John 1:29; 8:34–36; 1 John 1:7; 3:4–9; 5:18.

To complete the book of Romans during this twelve-part study, read Romans 6:1–23.

JOURNALING

What bad habits do I need to address? What changes do I need to make to live a more godly life?

LESSON SIX

NOT GUILTY

MAX
LUCADO

REFLECTION

Some days we can live in the truth of the freedom and forgiveness we have in Christ. Some days it's not so easy. We surprise ourselves by "caving in" to temptations we think we've left behind. But Romans tells us that we have been set free from sin and are no longer under condemnation! Do you ever wonder if God will continue to "let you off the hook" after sinning again? How do you deal with guilt and shame in your life?

SITUATION

Paul has brilliantly illuminated the message of our spiritual emancipation. We were slaves to sin; now we are free in Christ. But we still struggle. We are painfully aware of our human shortcomings and our tendency to betray what we know is right. How does God bring together our obvious instability with his unchanging nature and character? This chapter gives us an overwhelming picture of God's grand commitment to us.

OBSERVATION

Read Romans 8:1–17 in the NCV or the NKJV.

NCV

¹So now, those who are in Christ Jesus are not judged guilty. ²Through Christ Jesus the law of the Spirit that brings life made me free from the law that brings sin and death. ³The law was without power, because the law was made weak by our sinful selves. But God did what the law could not do. He sent his own Son to earth with the same human life that others use for sin. By sending his Son to be an offering to pay for sin, God used a human life to destroy sin. ⁴He did this so that we could be the kind of people the law correctly wants us to be. Now we do not live following our sinful selves, but we live following the Spirit.

⁵Those who live following their sinful selves think only about things that their sinful selves want. But those who live following the Spirit are thinking about the things the Spirit wants them to do. ⁶If people's thinking is controlled by the sinful self, there is death. But if their thinking is controlled by the Spirit, there is life and peace. ⁷When people's thinking is controlled by the sinful self, they are against God, because they refuse to obey God's law and really are not even able to obey God's law. ⁸Those people who are ruled by their sinful selves cannot please God.

⁹But you are not ruled by your sinful selves. You are ruled by the Spirit, if that Spirit of God really lives in you. But the person who does not have the Spirit of Christ does not belong to Christ. ¹⁰Your body will always be dead because of sin. But if Christ is in you, then the Spirit gives you life, because Christ made you right with God. ¹¹God raised Jesus from the dead, and if God's Spirit is living in you, he will also give life to your bodies that die. God is the One who raised Christ from the dead, and he will give life through his Spirit that lives in you.

¹²So, my brothers and sisters, we must not be ruled by our sinful selves or live the way our sinful selves want. ¹³If you use your lives to do the wrong things your sinful selves want, you will die spiritually. But if you use the Spirit's help to stop doing the wrong things you do with your body, you will have true life.

¹⁴The true children of God are those who let God's Spirit lead them. ¹⁵The Spirit we received does not make us slaves again to fear; it makes us children of God. With that Spirit we cry out, "Father." ¹⁶And the Spirit himself joins with our spirits to say we are God's children. ¹⁷If we are God's children, we will receive blessings from God together with Christ. But we must suffer as Christ suffered so that we will have glory as Christ has glory.

NKJV

¹There is therefore now no condemnation to those who are in Christ Jesus, who do not walk according to the flesh, but according to the Spirit. ²For the law of the Spirit of life in Christ Jesus has made me free from the law of sin and death. ³For what the law could not do in that it was weak through the flesh, God did by sending His own Son in the likeness of sinful flesh, on account of sin: He condemned sin in the flesh, ⁴that the righteous requirement of the law might be fulfilled in us who do not walk according to the flesh but according to the Spirit. ⁵For those who live according to the flesh set their minds on the things of the flesh, but those who live according to the Spirit, the things of the Spirit. ⁶For to be carnally minded is death, but to be spiritually minded is life and peace. ⁷Because the carnal mind is enmity against God; for it is not subject to the law of God, nor indeed can be. ⁸So then, those who are in the flesh cannot please God.

⁹But you are not in the flesh but in the Spirit, if indeed the Spirit of God dwells in you. Now if anyone does not have the Spirit of Christ, he is not His. ¹⁰And if Christ is in you, the body is dead because of sin, but the Spirit is life because of righteousness. ¹¹But if the Spirit of Him who raised Jesus from the dead dwells in you, He who raised Christ from the dead will also give life to your mortal bodies through His Spirit who dwells in you.

¹²Therefore, brethren, we are debtors—not to the flesh, to live according to the flesh. ¹³For if you live according to the flesh you will die; but if by the Spirit you put to death the deeds of the body, you will live. ¹⁴For as many as are led by the Spirit of God, these are sons of God. ¹⁵For you did not receive the spirit of bondage again to fear, but you received the Spirit of adoption by whom we cry out, "Abba, Father." ¹⁶The Spirit Himself bears witness with our spirit that we are children of God, ¹⁷and if children, then heirs—heirs of God and joint heirs with Christ, if indeed we suffer with Him, that we may also be glorified together.

EXPLORATION

1. Explain how the law as a list of rules and behavior standards cannot provide salvation.

2. According to this passage, who is unable to please God? Why?

3. In what ways does the Spirit of God transform people? [Note: The Spirit of God gives people new life (John 6:63; 2 Cor. 3:6); empowers believers for special tasks (Judg. 3.10), helps believers worship (John 4:23–24); enables believers to spread the gospel (Matt. 10:19–20); and guides, teaches and convicts people of sin (Luke 12:12; John 14:26; 16:7–13).]

4. How can a person attain true life?

5. Explain what it means to live by the Spirit.

INSPIRATION

Peter learned the lesson. But wouldn't you know it? Peter forgot the lesson. Two short years later this man who confessed Christ in the boat cursed Christ at a fire. The night before Jesus' crucifixion, Peter told people that he'd never heard of Jesus.

He couldn't have made a more tragic mistake. He knew it. The burly fisherman buried his bearded face in thick hands and spent Friday night in tears. All the feelings of that Galilean morning came back to him. *It's too late.*

But then Sunday came. Jesus came! Peter saw him. Peter was convinced that Christ had come back from the dead. But apparently Peter wasn't convinced that Christ came back for *him*. So he went back to the boat--to the same boat, the same beach, the same sea. He came out of retirement. He and his buddies washed the barnacles off the hull, unpacked the nets, and pushed out. They fished all night, and, honest to Pete, they caught nothing.

Poor Peter. Blew it as a disciple. Now he's blowing it as a fisherman. About the time he wonders it it's too late to take up carpentry, the sky turns orange, and they hear a voice from the coastline, "Had any luck?"

They yell back, "No."

"Try the right side of the boat!"

With nothing to lose and no more pride to protect, they give it a go. "So they cast, and then they were not able to haul it in because of the great number of fish" (John 21:6 NASB). It takes a moment for the déjà vu to hit Peter. But when he does, he cannonballs into the water and swims as fast as he can to see the one who loved him enough to *re-create* a miracle. This time the message stuck.

Peter never again fished for fish. He spent the rest of his days telling anyone who would listen, "It's not too late to try again."

Is it too late for you? Before you say yes, before you fold up the nets and head for the house—two questions. *Have you given Christ your boat?* Your heartache? Your dead-end dilemma? Your struggle? Have you really turned it over to him? *And have you gone deep?* Have you bypassed the surface-water solutions you can see in search of the deep-channel provisions God can give? Try the other side of the boat. (From *Next Door Savior* by Max Lucado)

REACTION

6. How does the truth of this Bible passage and the parallel reflection above motivate you to live your life?

7. How has your life changed since you began your new life in Christ?

8. How should believers deal with feelings of condemnation and guilt?

9. What new perspective does this study give you about Christ's sacrifice?

10. What evidence of the Holy Spirit's control can people see in your life?

11. In what areas do you need to depend more on the Holy Spirit and less on your own desires?

LIFE LESSONS

Wanting to give up is not all that uncommon, even for Christians. Feeling like a failure is familiar territory for all of us. But this part of God's Word makes it clear that quitting is not an option. Nothing will separate us from God's love. The Holy Spirit will help us go on and live in the freedom of forgiveness. He will show us what it means to "try the other side of the boat" in our lives.

DEVOTION

Father, we want to come to you, but sometimes we are too ashamed of who we are and what we have done. We're afraid that we have done something unforgivable, afraid that you will reject us. But Father, your Word teaches us that you sacrificed your Son as the atonement for our sin. There is no sin too deep for your hand of forgiveness to reach. Thank you, Father, for the assurance that we are forgiven and acceptable in your sight.

For more Bible passages on Christ's sacrifice for sin, see John 1:29; Romans 3:25; 2 Corinthians 5:21; Hebrews 9:26–28; 10:19–22; 1 Peter 2:24; 1 John 2:2; 4:10.

To complete the book of Romans during this twelve-part study, read Romans 7:1–8:39.

JOURNALING

How do I feel about being judged "not guilty" by God?

GOD'S
PERFECT
PLAN

MAX
LUCADO

REFLECTION

Some people are exposed to the message of salvation through Jesus Christ hundreds of times without ever really hearing it. The good news is lost among many other messages with little purpose or hope. Others seem to respond the first time they hear about Christ. Who told you about Jesus and the gospel message of salvation? What was your initial response?

SITUATION

The apostle Paul was deeply aware that he was walking on holy ground with his writings. The Jewish history he used to illustrate God's amazing plan of grace for the whole world was the same history that the Jewish people used as proof of being God's exclusive people. Paul felt great love for his fellow Israelites, and even wished that he could take their place under God's judgment if it would ensure their understanding of the gospel. Now he highlights the ongoing plans for Israel, God's chosen people.

OBSERVATION

Read Romans 10:1–15 in the NCV or the NKJV.

NCV

¹Brothers and sisters, the thing I want most is for all the Jews to be saved. That is my prayer to God. ²I can say this about them: They really try to follow God, but they do not know the right way. ³Because they did not know the way that God makes people right with him, they tried to make themselves right in their own way. So they did not accept God's way of making people right. ⁴Christ ended the law so that everyone who believes in him may be right with God.

⁵*Moses writes about being made right by following the law. He says, "A person who obeys these things will live because of them." ⁶But this is what the Scripture says about being made right through faith: "Don't say to yourself, 'Who will go up into heaven?'" (That means, "Who will go up to heaven and bring Christ down to earth?") ⁷"And do not say, 'Who will go down into the world below?'" (That means, "Who will go down and bring Christ up from the dead?") ⁸This is what the Scripture says: "The word is near you; it is in your mouth and in your heart." That is the teaching of faith that we are telling. ⁹If you use your mouth to say, "Jesus is Lord," and if you believe in your heart that God raised Jesus from the dead, you will be saved. ¹⁰We believe with our hearts, and so we are made right with God. And we use our mouths to say that we believe, and so we are saved. ¹¹As the Scripture says, "Anyone who trusts in him will never be disappointed." ¹²That Scripture says "anyone" because there is no difference between those who are Jews and those who are not. The same Lord is the Lord of all and gives many blessings to all who trust in him, ¹³as the Scripture says, "Anyone who calls on the Lord will be saved."*

¹⁴*But before people can ask the Lord for help, they must believe in him; and before they can believe in him, they must hear about him; and for them to hear about the Lord, someone must tell them; ¹⁵and before someone can go and tell them, that person must be sent. It is written, "How beautiful is the person who comes to bring good news."*

NKJV

¹*Brethren, my heart's desire and prayer to God for Israel is that they may be saved. ²For I bear them witness that they have a zeal for God, but not according to knowledge. ³For they being ignorant of God's righteousness, and seeking to establish their own righteousness, have not submitted to the righteousness of God. ⁴For Christ is the end of the law for righteousness to everyone who believes.*

⁵*For Moses writes about the righteousness which is of the law, "The man who does those things shall live by them." ⁶But the righteousness of faith speaks in this way, "Do not say in your heart, 'Who will ascend into heaven?'" (that is, to bring Christ down from above) ⁷or, "'Who will descend into the abyss?'" (that is, to bring Christ up from the dead). ⁸But what does it say? "The word is near you, in your mouth and in your heart" (that is, the word of faith which we preach): ⁹that if you confess with your mouth the Lord Jesus and believe in your heart that God has raised Him from the dead, you will be saved. ¹⁰For with the heart one believes unto righteousness, and with the mouth confession is made unto salvation. ¹¹For the Scripture says, "Whoever believes on Him will not be put to shame." ¹²For there is no distinction between Jew and Greek, for the same Lord over all is rich to all who call upon Him. ¹³For "whoever calls on the name of the LORD shall be saved."*

¹⁴*How then shall they call on Him in whom they have not believed? And how shall they believe in Him of whom they have not heard? And how shall they hear without a preacher? ¹⁵And how shall they preach unless they are sent? As it is written:*

"How beautiful are the feet of those who preach the gospel of peace,

Who bring glad tidings of good things!"

EXPLORATION

1. What is wrong with trying to be saved your own way?

2. What part do our thoughts and our words have in our response to salvation?

3. What promise is given to people who believe and confess that Jesus is Lord?

4. How does God's righteousness motivate us to godly behavior?

5. What does this passage teach about the way the good news is spread, understood, and accepted? [Note: Romans 10:14–15 emphasizes the importance of spreading the gospel message. It's tempting to assume that these verses were written to evangelists and pastors, but every believer is responsible to share the good news. (See 2 Kings 7:9; Matthew 9:35–38; 28:18–20; and Acts 1:8.)]

INSPIRATION

The Bible teaches that God was a God of love. He wanted to do something for man. He wanted to save man. He wanted to free man from the curse of sin. How could He do it? God was a just God. He was righteous, and holy. He had warned man from the beginning that if he obeyed the Devil and disobeyed God, he would die physically and spiritually . . .

All through the Old Testament, God gave man the promise of salvation if by faith he would believe in the coming Redeemer. Therefore God began to teach His people that man could only be saved by substitution. Someone else would have to pay the bill for man's redemption . . .

Thanks be to God—that is exactly what happened! Looking down over the battlements of heaven He saw this planet swinging in space—doomed, damned, crushed, and bound for hell. He saw you and me struggling beneath our load of sin and bound in the chains and ropes of sin. He made His decision in the council halls of God. The angelic hosts bowed in humility and awe as heaven's Prince of Princes and Lord of Lords, who could speak worlds into space, got into His jeweled chariot, went through pearly gates, across the steep of the skies, and on a black Judean night, while the stars sang together and the escorting angels chanted praises, stepped out of the chariot, threw off His robes, and became man! (From *Peace with God* by Billy Graham)

REACTION

6. What aspects of God's character are shown through his plan of salvation?

7. How are you encouraged by God's plan to save the world?

8. Why is it difficult for us to follow Jesus?

9. What can we learn from Israel's response to God's plan of salvation?

10. How can you guard against trying to earn God's approval and acceptance?

11. Why is it important to tell others about your faith in Jesus Christ? Someone (maybe even several people) went out of his or her way to communicate the gospel to you. How does your effort to pass on the message demonstrate your appreciation for the efforts that were made on your behalf?

LIFE LESSONS

God's perfect plan involves a two-part response from us: internal belief and external behavior. We accept with our hearts and confess with our mouths (10:9). Genuine faith always involves both the inside and outside. It is not just a public formality or a private belief; it's both. And once it begins; it continues. The internal response connects us with God; the external one confirms our belief and gives others the opportunity to experience the same benefits of God's plan that we have received.

DEVOTION

Father, help us understand that your plan is based on love—not on our performance. Help us to be captivated by your love. To be overwhelmed by your grace. To come home to you in that beautiful path that you've already carved out for us.

For more Bible passages on God's plan of salvation, see John 3:16; 4:22; Acts 4:12; 28:28; 2 Corinthians 7:10; 1 Thessalonians 5:9; Revelation 7:10.

To complete the book of Romans during this twelve-part study, read Romans 9:1–10:21.

JOURNALING

How can my external life reflect more of the internal realities of my salvation?

CALLED BY GOD

MAX LUCADO

REFLECTION

Think of a time when you were given a special honor or privilege. Perhaps someone unexpectedly acknowledged a service you rendered. Maybe one of your children took time to express their appreciation, or your boss rewarded you in some way. How did that recognition make you feel? Now think about the honor of being recognized and called by God. How does that make you feel?

SITUATION

In this chapter Paul includes references about well-known Old Testament figures to illustrate God's larger plan. Elijah's appeal to God is recorded in 1 Kings 19:10–18. The prophet Isaiah's prediction that God would punish hardhearted people is found in Isaiah 6:9–13. Romans 11:8 is based on Deuteronomy 29:4 and Isaiah 29:10. Paul continues to encourage his Jewish and Gentile audience to see that God's plan and offer of salvation ultimately includes all of them.

OBSERVATION

Read Romans 11:1–15 in the NCV or the NKJV.

NCV

¹So I ask: Did God throw out his people? No! I myself am an Israelite from the family of Abraham, from the tribe of Benjamin. ²God chose the Israelites to be his people before they were born, and he has not thrown his people out. Surely you know what the Scripture says about Elijah, how he prayed to God against the people of Israel. ³"Lord," he said, "they have killed your prophets, and they have destroyed your altars. I am the only prophet left, and now they are trying to kill me, too." ⁴But what answer did God give Elijah? He said, "But I have left seven thousand people in Israel who have never bowed down before Baal." ⁵It is the same now. There are a few people that God has chosen by his grace. ⁶And if he chose them by grace, it is not for the things they have done. If they could be made God's people by what they did, God's gift of grace would not really be a gift.

[7]So this is what has happened: Although the Israelites tried to be right with God, they did not succeed, but the ones God chose did become right with him. The others were made stubborn and refused to listen to God. [8]As it is written in the Scriptures:

"God gave the people a dull mind so

they could not understand."

"He closed their eyes so they could not see

and their ears so they could not hear.

This continues until today."

[9]And David says:

"Let their own feasts trap them and

cause their ruin;

let their feasts cause them to stumble

and be paid back.

[10]Let their eyes be closed so they cannot see

and their backs be forever weak from troubles."

[11]So I ask: When the Jews fell, did that fall destroy them? No! But their mistake brought salvation to those who are not Jews, in order to make the Jews jealous. [12]The Jews' mistake brought rich blessings for the world, and the Jews' loss brought rich blessings for the non-Jewish people. So surely the world will receive much richer blessings when enough Jews become the kind of people God wants.

[13]Now I am speaking to you who are not Jews. I am an apostle to those who are not Jews, and since I have that work, I will make the most of it. [14]I hope I can make my own people jealous and, in that way, help some of them to be saved. [15]When God turned away from the Jews, he became friends with other people in the world. So when God accepts the Jews, surely that will bring them life after death.

NKJV

[1]I say then, has God cast away His people? Certainly not! For I also am an Israelite, of the seed of Abraham, of the tribe of Benjamin. [2]God has not cast away His people whom He foreknew. Or do you not know what the Scripture says of Elijah, how he pleads with God against Israel, saying, [3]"LORD, they have killed Your prophets and torn down Your altars, and I alone am left, and they seek my life"? [4]But what does the divine response say to him? "I have reserved for Myself seven thousand men who have not bowed the knee to Baal." [5]Even so then, at this present time there is a remnant according to the election of grace. [6]And if by grace, then it is no longer of works; otherwise grace is no longer grace. But if it is of works, it is no longer grace; otherwise work is no longer work.

[7]What then? Israel has not obtained what it seeks; but the elect have obtained it, and the rest were blinded. [8]Just as it is written:

"God has given them a spirit of stupor,

Eyes that they should not see

And ears that they should not hear,

To this very day."

⁹And David says:

"Let their table become a snare and a trap,

A stumbling block and a recompense to them.

¹⁰ Let their eyes be darkened, so that they do not see,

And bow down their back always."

¹¹I say then, have they stumbled that they should fall? Certainly not! But through their fall, to provoke them to jealousy, salvation has come to the Gentiles. ¹²Now if their fall is riches for the world, and their failure riches for the Gentiles, how much more their fullness!

¹³For I speak to you Gentiles; inasmuch as I am an apostle to the Gentiles, I magnify my ministry, ¹⁴if by any means I may provoke to jealousy those who are my flesh and save some of them. ¹⁵For if their being cast away is the reconciling of the world, what will their acceptance be but life from the dead?

EXPLORATION

1. Why did people think that God must have rejected the Israelites?

2. What does God's answer to Elijah show us?

3. How do people try to earn God's grace? Why don't our efforts put God in our debt?

4. Why are some people open to the good news and others are closed?

5. Why can we be confident that God's grace is for all who will receive it?

INSPIRATION

The fact that God has chosen some to be saved does not mean that He has chosen the rest to be lost. The world is already lost and dead in sins. If left to ourselves, all of us would be condemned eternally. The question is, Does God have a right to stoop down, take a handful of already doomed clay, and fashion a vessel of beauty out of it? Of course He does. C. R. Erdman put it in the right perspective when he said, "God's sovereignty is never exercised in condemning men who ought to be saved, but rather it has resulted in the salvation of men who ought to be lost."

The only way people can know if they are among the elect is by trusting Jesus Christ as Lord and Savior (1 Thess. 1:4–7). God holds people responsible to accept the Savior by an act of the will. In reproving those Jews who did not believe, Jesus placed the blame on their will. He did *not* say, "You cannot come to Me because you are not chosen." Rather, He *did* say, "You *are not willing* to come to Me that you may have life" (John 5:40 NKJV, emphasis added).

The real question of a believer is not, Does the sovereign God have the right to choose people to be saved? Rather it is, Why did He choose *me*? This should make a person a worshiper for all eternity. (From *Alone in Majesty* by William MacDonald)

REACTION

6. What hope does God offer to all people?

7. What can you learn from this passage about God's sovereignty and our responsibility?

8. What things does this passage make you feel grateful for?

9. How do you think some people are misled about the true way of salvation?

10. In what different things do people put their hope for salvation?

11. Why is it important that we not take our salvation for granted?

LIFE LESSONS

As tempting as it may be at times to ask, "Am I called by God?" the real question that needs to be answered is, "Have I answered God's invitation?" The emphasis we put on one or the other of these questions says a lot about how we think of God. Is God someone who wants to keep us in the dark or someone who has gone to great lengths to bring us into the light? Does he want us to live in doubt or live by faith? If we let God take care of the calling and we focus on the way we respond to him from day to day, we will experience a growing awareness of his voice, speaking powerfully through his Word.

DEVOTION

O Sovereign God, you are beyond our understanding. Your ways are perfect; your unlimited mercy astounds us. Thank you for calling us to yourself and claiming us for your own. Teach us to trust you more, to love you deeply, and to turn to you in humility every day.

For more Bible passages on the way God chooses to save, see Deuteronomy 9:4–5; Romans 2:4; 8:28–29; Ephesians 1:4–6, 11; 2:8–9; 1 Timothy 2:3–4; Titus 3:4–5.

To complete the book of Romans during this twelve-part study, read Romans 11:1–36.

JOURNALING

In what specific ways have I responded to God's call on my life?

LESSON NINE

ONE BODY, MANY PARTS

MAX LUCADO

REFLECTION

Some of God's best gifts are relationships with people who show us the gritty and practical sides of following Jesus Christ. These people really *live!* They are not stereotypical, and yet they remind us of Jesus. They break the mold, yet they illustrate God's image. With hardly a word they provoke us to live better, to sacrifice, to pay closer attention. Their transformed lives direct us to be more like Christ. Have you met anyone like that recently? What gifts or abilities in that person do you most appreciate? How have you let him or her know your gratitude?

SITUATION

In most of his letters, the apostle Paul spends the first half laying a foundation of teaching. Then he switches to a closing section of application. Romans is no exception. He begins this epistle with *What we believe* and concludes with *Therefore, what does it mean?* Paul is saying, "Now that you've grasped these foundational truths, here's how to live them out."

OBSERVATION

Read Romans 12:1–13 in the NCV or the NKJV.

NCV

¹So brothers and sisters, since God has shown us great mercy, I beg you to offer your lives as a living sacrifice to him. Your offering must be only for God and pleasing to him, which is the spiritual way for you to worship. ²Do not change yourselves to be like the people of this world, but be changed within by a new way of thinking. Then you will be able to decide what God wants for you; you will know what is good and pleasing to him and what is perfect. ³Because God has given me a special gift, I have something to say to everyone among you. Do not think you are better than you are. You must decide what you really are by the amount of faith God has given you. ⁴Each one of us has a body with many parts, and these parts all have different uses. ⁵In the same way, we are many, but in Christ we are all one body. Each one is a part of that body, and each part belongs to all the other parts. ⁶We all have different gifts, each of which came because of the grace God gave us. The person who has the gift of prophecy should use that gift in agreement with the faith. ⁷Anyone who has the gift of serving should serve. Anyone who has the gift of teaching should teach. ⁸Whoever has the gift of encouraging others should encourage. Whoever has the gift of giving to others should give freely. Anyone who has the gift of being a leader should try hard when he leads. Whoever has the gift of showing mercy to others should do so with joy.

⁹Your love must be real. Hate what is evil, and hold on to what is good. ¹⁰Love each other like brothers and sisters. Give each other more honor than you want for yourselves. ¹¹Do not be lazy but work hard, serving the Lord with all your heart. ¹²Be joyful because you have hope. Be patient when trouble comes, and pray at all times. ¹³Share with God's people who need help. Bring strangers in need into your homes.

NKJV

¹I beseech you therefore, brethren, by the mercies of God, that you present your bodies a living sacrifice, holy, acceptable to God, which is your reasonable service. ²And do not be conformed to this world, but be transformed by the renewing of your mind, that you may prove what is that good and acceptable and perfect will of God.

³For I say, through the grace given to me, to everyone who is among you, not to think of himself more highly than he ought to think, but to think soberly, as God has dealt to each one a measure of faith. ⁴For as we have many members in one body, but all the members do not have the same function, ⁵so we, being many, are one body in Christ, and individually members of one another. ⁶Having then gifts differing according to the grace that is given to us, let us use them: if prophecy, let us prophesy in proportion to our faith; ⁷or ministry, let us use it in our ministering; he who teaches, in teaching; ⁸he who exhorts, in exhortation; he who gives, with liberality; he who leads, with diligence; he who shows mercy, with cheerfulness.

⁹Let love be without hypocrisy. Abhor what is evil. Cling to what is good. ¹⁰Be kindly affectionate to one another with brotherly love, in honor giving preference to one another; ¹¹not lagging in diligence, fervent in spirit, serving the Lord; ¹²rejoicing in hope, patient in tribulation, continuing steadfastly in prayer; ¹³distributing to the needs of the saints, given to hospitality.

EXPLORATION

1. What does it mean to be a living sacrifice? (Consider the following statement: "The only problem with a living sacrifice is that it keeps crawling off the altar.")

2. What does Paul mean when he tells us to be "changed within by a new way of thinking" (12:2 NCV)?

3. What hinders Christians from thinking and acting like parts of one body?

4. What advice does this passage offer about getting along with one another in the body of Christ?

5. Based on this passage, what basic guidelines should govern how we react during ordinary times and during times of trouble (vv. 11–12)?

INSPIRATION

Accept your part in his plan. God uses people like Bob Russell to illustrate this kind of love. Bob ministers at the Southeast Christian Church in Louisville, Kentucky. When Bob began his service there in 1966, the church had 125 members, and Bob was twenty-two years old. During the last three and a half decades, God has built this church into one of his finest and largest families. Over 16,000 people gather each weekend to worship in one of several services.

In 1989 Bob made a choice that surprised many observers. He announced that he was going to share the preaching duties with a twenty-seven-year-old preacher. He and Dave Stone would begin coministering to the church. In the announced plan, each year Bob would preach less and Dave would preach more, thus providing Bob more time to lead the church and the church an experienced successor.

Not everyone could do that. Larger egos in smaller churches have struggled to surrender the pulpit. But Bob understands the danger of the pecking order and is humble enough to invert it.

True humility is not thinking lowly of yourself but thinking accurately of yourself. The humble heart does not say, "I can't do anything." But rather, "I can't do everything. I know my part and am happy to do it."

When Paul writes "*consider* others better than yourselves" (Phil. 2:3 NIV, emphasis mine), he uses a verb that means "to calculate," "to reckon." The word implies a conscious judgment resting on carefully weighed facts. To consider others better than yourself, then, is not to say you have no place; it is to say that you know your place. "Don't cherish exaggerated ideas of yourself or your importance, but try to have a sane estimate of your capabilities by the light of the faith that God has given to you" (Rom. 12:3 PHILLIPS). (From *A Love Worth Giving* by Max Lucado)

REACTION

6. Why is it difficult to resist comparing ourselves with other believers, or wishing we had their "role" in the body of Christ?

7. How hard is it for you to be patient when your abilities don't seem to be needed, or you're having a hard time fitting in to the local church body? Why?

8. List some areas of your life where you need to be more patient.

9. How is it possible for troubles to be a blessing?

10. Based on this passage, what spiritual gifts do you think God has given you?

11. What does it mean to be "transformed" and serve God with all your heart?

LIFE LESSONS

The challenge for a follower of Jesus is never as much what to do as where to start. We lack obedience more than guidance. There are always enough general commands from God to keep us busy for a lifetime. Obeying what we know usually leads to clarity about what we don't know. Most of what God instructs us to put into action doesn't require that we go somewhere else to practice. We can start practicing love, peacemaking, and patience right where we are. These often help us identify our gifts and roles in the body.

DEVOTION

God of peace, teach us what it means to be peacemakers. Help us to cultivate peace between others and you—in our churches, neighborhoods, offices, and schoolrooms. Help us to start today, in whatever circumstance we find ourselves. Teach us to rely on you to defend us instead of constantly sticking up for ourselves. Teach us the art of building bridges and not walls. May we be slow to judge and quick to forgive. Don't let us put off what we can do today.

For more Bible passages on identifying your spiritual gifts and learning how to use them for the encouragement of other Christians, see 1 Corinthians 12:12–31; 14:1–40; and Ephesians 4:1–16.

To complete the book of Romans during this twelve-part study, read Romans 12:1–21.

JOURNALING

How can you offer yourself and your spiritual gifts as a living sacrifice to God?

LESSON TEN

TRUE LOVE

MAX
LUCADO

REFLECTION

"All you need is love" the song goes. That may be true, but most people look for it in the wrong places. Since God is the original source and inexhaustible supply of love, those who know God should function as channels for his love in the world. Think of a time when a friend showed love for you in a special way. How did that make you feel? How did you respond? In what ways did you experience God's love through that expression of love?

SITUATION

The last section of Romans includes Paul's teaching on the way followers of Jesus should behave in the church, as well as giving instruction about how to relate to the society we live in. These instructions talk about how to respond to hostility from the world and the duties of citizenship. Then Paul reiterates the power of love. In this passage he describes the nature of authentic love, a love that all who serve Christ should exhibit.

OBSERVATION

Read Romans 13:8–14 in the NCV or the NKJV.

NCV

⁸Do not owe people anything, except always owe love to each other, because the person who loves others has obeyed all the law. ⁹The law says, "You must not be guilty of adultery. You must not murder anyone. You must not steal. You must not want to take your neighbor's things." All these commands and all others are really only one rule: "Love your neighbor as you love yourself." ¹⁰Love never hurts a neighbor, so loving is obeying all the law.

¹¹Do this because we live in an important time. It is now time for you to wake up from your sleep, because our salvation is nearer now than when we first believed. ¹²The "night" is almost finished, and the "day" is almost here. So we should stop doing things that belong to darkness and take up the weapons used for fighting in the light. ¹³Let us live in a right way, like people who belong to the day. We should not have wild parties or get drunk. There should be no sexual sins of any kind, no fighting or jealousy. ¹⁴But clothe yourselves with the Lord Jesus Christ and forget about satisfying your sinful self.

NKJV

⁸Owe no one anything except to love one another, for he who loves another has fulfilled the law. ⁹For the commandments, "You shall not commit adultery," "You shall not murder," "You shall not steal," "You shall not bear false witness," "You shall not covet," and if there is any other commandment, are all summed up in this saying, namely, "You shall love your neighbor as yourself." ¹⁰Love does no harm to a neighbor; therefore love is the fulfillment of the law.

¹¹And do this, knowing the time, that now it is high time to awake out of sleep; for now our salvation is nearer than when we first believed. ¹²The night is far spent, the day is at hand. Therefore let us cast off the works of darkness, and let us put on the armor of light. ¹³Let us walk properly, as in the day, not in revelry and drunkenness, not in lewdness and lust, not in strife and envy. ¹⁴But put on the Lord Jesus Christ, and make no provision for the flesh, to fulfill its lusts.

EXPLORATION

1. What is the one debt we are to owe to one another? In what sense is this a "debt"?

2. What one rule does Paul say sums up the whole law?

3. Write in your own words how this passage describes true love.

4. What does Paul mean when he describes believers as "people who belong to the day"?

5. How can we "put on" or "clothe" ourselves with the Lord Jesus? (Passages like Galatians 3:26–27; Ephesians 4:22–24; and Colossians 3:9–17 may offer some insight.)

INSPIRATION

You know your love is real when you weep with those who weep and rejoice with those who rejoice. You know your love is real when you feel for others what Catherine Lawes felt for the inmates of Sing Sing prison. When her husband, Lewis, became the warden in 1921, she was a young mother of three daughters. Everybody warned her to never step foot inside the walls. But she didn't listen to them. When the first prison basketball game was held, in she went, three girls in tow, and took a seat in the bleachers with the inmates.

She once said, "My husband and I are going to take care of these men, and I believe they will take care of me! I don't have to worry!"

When she heard that one convicted murderer was blind, she taught him Braille so he could read. Upon learning of inmates who were hearing impaired, she studied sign language so they could communicate. For sixteen years Catherine Lewis softened the hard hearts of the men of Sing Sing. In 1937 the world saw the difference real love makes.

The prisoners knew something was wrong when Lewis Lawes didn't report to work. Quickly the word spread that Catherine had been killed in a car accident. The following day her body was placed in her home, three quarters of a mile from the prison. As the acting warden took his early morning walk, he noticed a large gathering at the main gate. Every prisoner pressed against the fence. Eyes awash with tears. Faces solemn. No one spoke or moved. They'd come to stand as close as they could to the woman who'd given them love.

The warden made a remarkable decision. "All right, men, you can go. Just be sure to check in tonight." These were America's hardest criminals. Murderers. Robbers. These men the nation had locked away for life. But the warden unlocked the gate for them, and they walked without an escort or guard to the home of Catherine Lawes to pay their last respects. And to a man, each one returned.

Real love changes people. (From *A Love Worth Giving* by Max Lucado)

REACTION

6. What are some of the misconceptions people have about love?

7. How is God's view of love different from the world's view? (Note: Learn more about God's view of love by reading Jeremiah 31:3; John 3:16; 14:15; 16:27; Romans 5:8; 1 Corinthians 13:1–13; Ephesians 2:4–5; and 1 John 3:1; 4:7–21.)

8. Why is it important that we love others?

9. How do you usually respond to the "unlovable people" in our society?

10. In what ways do you demonstrate your love for your friends?

11. Think of a person who needs to feel God's love. How can you demonstrate God's love to that person?

LIFE LESSONS

When Jesus was asked to summarize the purpose of life, he immediately focused on loving God and loving our neighbor. He stated what Paul echoed in this passage: that genuine love automatically covers the rest of God's commands. This is not a self-centered, little-more-than-emotions love. The goal is God's kind of unconditional love. Once we've learned to love God's way, the other challenges of life will fall into place.

DEVOTION

God, help us to show your love to those around us. Open our eyes to people who are in desperate need of a loving touch. Let our lives be testimonies of your love for us, so that when people see us, they will feel your love for them.

For more Bible passages on loving others, see John 15:9–13; 1 Corinthians 13; Galatians 5:13–14; Ephesians 5:1–2; Colossians 3:12–14; 1 Peter 1:22; 1 John 3:11–23; 4:7–8.

To complete the book of Romans during this twelve-part study, read Romans 13:1–14.

JOURNALING

What motivates me to love others? What prevents me from loving others?

ACCEPTING ONE ANOTHER

MAX
LUCADO

REFLECTION

It could be said that the degree of peace in any situation is directly proportionate to the degree that each participant is willing to compromise. Peace always involves sacrifice. Peace requires people to willingly consider the interests of others as well as their own. Describe a particular time when you sensed a spirit of unity among Christians. In what sense was that true peace, and how was it maintained?

SITUATION

Throughout the epistle of Romans, Paul has delivered a fountain of pithy and practical guidelines for spiritual living. His counsel alternates between choices and actions by individuals on the one hand, and the well-being of the body of Christ on the other. He celebrates freedom in Christ, but cautions against a tendency to make freedom the end in itself, rather than a means to an end. God's freedom is not a license to do anything we want, but a charge to always consider what is best for others.

OBSERVATION

Read Romans 14:13–23 in the NCV or the NKJV.

NCV

¹³For that reason we should stop judging each other. We must make up our minds not to do anything that will make another Christian sin. ¹⁴I am in the Lord Jesus, and I know that there is no food that is wrong to eat. But if a person believes something is wrong, that thing is wrong for him. ¹⁵If you hurt your brother's or sister's faith because of something you eat, you are not really following the way of love. Do not destroy someone's faith by eating food he thinks is wrong, because Christ died for him. ¹⁶Do not allow what you think is good to become what others say is evil. ¹⁷In the kingdom of God, eating and drinking are not important. The important things are living right with God, peace, and joy in the Holy Spirit. ¹⁸Anyone who serves Christ by living this way is pleasing God and will be accepted by other people.

¹⁹So let us try to do what makes peace and helps one another. ²⁰Do not let the eating of food destroy the work of God. All foods are all right to eat, but it is wrong to eat food that causes someone else to sin. ²¹It is better not to eat meat or drink wine or do anything that will cause your brother or sister to sin.

²²Your beliefs about these things should be kept secret between you and God. People are happy if they can do what they think is right without feeling guilty. ²³But those who eat something without being sure it is right are wrong because they did not believe it was right. Anything that is done without believing it is right is a sin.

NKJV

¹³Therefore let us not judge one another anymore, but rather resolve this, not to put a stumbling block or a cause to fall in our brother's way.

¹⁴I know and am convinced by the Lord Jesus that there is nothing unclean of itself; but to him who considers anything to be unclean, to him it is unclean. ¹⁵Yet if your brother is grieved because of your food, you are no longer walking in love. Do not destroy with your food the one for whom Christ died. ¹⁶Therefore do not let your good be spoken of as evil; ¹⁷for the kingdom of God is not eating and drinking, but righteousness and peace and joy in the Holy Spirit. ¹⁸For he who serves Christ in these things is acceptable to God and approved by men.

¹⁹Therefore let us pursue the things which make for peace and the things by which one may edify another. ²⁰Do not destroy the work of God for the sake of food. All things indeed are pure, but it is evil for the man who eats with offense. ²¹It is good neither to eat meat nor drink wine nor do anything by which your brother stumbles or is offended or is made weak. ²²Do you have faith? Have it to yourself before God. Happy is he who does not condemn himself in what he approves. ²³But he who doubts is condemned if he eats, because he does not eat from faith; for whatever is not from faith is sin.

EXPLORATION

1. What issues caused division among the believers in Rome?

2. How did Paul counsel the Roman believers to deal with these issues?

3. What is the key point that Paul made in this passage? This debate over eating food offered to idols may not seem relevant today. But what is the timeless truth of Romans 14:17 that applies in any situation, even though the issues may change?

4. When should Christians defer to a fellow believer's beliefs?

5. Explain why it is more important to maintain unity than to maintain our personal rights.

INSPIRATION

Accepting others is basic to letting them be. The problem [in Paul's day] was not a meat problem; it was a love problem, an acceptance problem. It still is. How often we restrict our love by making it conditional: "If you will (or won't), then I will accept you." Paul starts there: "Accept one another!" . . . Those who didn't eat [meat] (called here "weak in the faith" in Romans 14:1 NKJV) were exhorted to accept and not judge those who ate. And those who ate were exhorted to accept and not regard with contempt those who did not eat. The secret lies in accepting one another. All of this is fairly easy to read so long as I stay on the issue of eating meat. That one is safe because it isn't a current taboo. It's easy to accept those folks today because they don't exist!

How about those in our life who may disagree with us on issues that are taboos in evangelical Christian circles today? Going to movies . . . playing cards . . . not having a "quiet time" every morning . . . going to a restaurant that sells liquor . . . listening to certain music . . . dancing . . . drinking coffee . . . In various areas of our country or the world, some or all of these things may be taboo . . . Remember, our goal is acceptance, the basis of a grace state of mind. (From *The Grace Awakening* by Charles Swindoll)

REACTION

6. What issues cause debates among Christians you know? (The point of this question and the next two is not to launch into one of those debates, but simply to raise the issues that are creating present controversies.)

7. How can believers handle controversial issues in a way that builds up the church rather than harms it?

8. How can believers show love and acceptance to one another, in spite of differing opinions on certain issues?

9. In your opinion, what are some issues that are not worth fighting over?

10. What beliefs are you not willing to compromise?

11. How can you avoid causing fellow believers to stumble in their faith?

LIFE LESSONS

Paul forces us to ask what's more important: getting our way or living God's way? The cultural surface issues shift constantly, but the underlying ones remain. Will we let God help us love one another despite our tendencies not to do so? Will we make freedom mean simply pursuing our desires or a means to pursue God's desires? Ultimately, we must recognize Christ's Lordship over even our freedom.

DEVOTION

We ask you, Father, to protect your church. Keep us from making our personal rights more important than the unity of your church. Keep us focused on the important things, the things that will build your kingdom. Give us the strength to love and accept one another. Bind us together through your Holy Spirit.

For more Bible passages on accepting others, see Matthew 7:1–5; Romans 15:7; 1 Corinthians 4:5; Galatians 2:6; James 4:12.

To complete the book of Romans during this twelve-part study, read Romans 14:1–15:13.

JOURNALING

How can I be more sensitive to the beliefs of my Christian friends?

LET IT SHINE

MAX
LUCADO

REFLECTION

Christians have a less-than-stellar reputation for handling conflicts and confrontations. We find it hard to speak the truth in love and to love truthfully. But most of us have benefited from watching someone who knew how to balance truth with genuine love. How has the positive example of another believer handling conflict well encouraged you?

SITUATION

This final passage of our study of Romans represents a beautiful example of Paul's practicing what he preached. As he concludes his letter, he wants to emphasize the high regard he has for those who will read it. He expresses his confidence that they can handle the hard-edged and serious parts of his letter. He reminds them of the main themes of God's glorious plan for the gospel and that God has their best interests at heart.

OBSERVATION

Read Romans 15:14–21 in the NCV or the NKJV.

NCV

14My brothers and sisters, I am sure that you are full of goodness. I know that you have all the knowledge you need and that you are able to teach each other. 15But I have written to you very openly about some things I wanted you to remember. I did this because God gave me this special gift: 16to be a minister of Christ Jesus to those who are not Jews. I served God by teaching his Good News, so that the non-Jewish people could be an offering that God would accept—an offering made holy by the Holy Spirit.

17So I am proud of what I have done for God in Christ Jesus. 18I will not talk about anything except what Christ has done through me in leading those who are not Jews to obey God. They have obeyed God because of what I have said and done, 19because of the power of miracles and the great things they saw, and because of the power of the Holy Spirit. I preached the Good News from Jerusalem all the way around to Illyricum, and so I have finished that part of my work. 20I always want to preach the Good News in places where people have never heard of Christ, because I do not want to build on the work someone else has already started. 21But it is written in the Scriptures:

"Those who were not told about him will see,

and those who have not heard about him will understand."

NKJV

14Now I myself am confident concerning you, my brethren, that you also are full of goodness, filled with all knowledge, able also to admonish one another. 15Nevertheless, brethren, I have written more boldly to you on some points, as reminding you, because of the grace given to me by God, 16that I might be a minister of Jesus Christ to the Gentiles, ministering the gospel of God, that the offering of the Gentiles might be acceptable, sanctified by the Holy Spirit. 17Therefore I have reason to glory in Christ Jesus in the things which pertain to God. 18For I will not dare to speak of any of those things which Christ has not accomplished through me, in word and deed, to make the Gentiles obedient—19in mighty signs and wonders, by the power of the Spirit of God, so that from Jerusalem and round about to Illyricum I have fully preached the gospel of Christ. 20And so I have made it my aim to preach the gospel, not where Christ was named, lest I should build on another man's foundation, 21but as it is written:

"To whom He was not announced, they shall see;

And those who have not heard shall understand."

EXPLORATION

1. What was the basis of Paul's confidence in the Christians in Rome?

2. List some of the things God had accomplished through Paul's life.

3. What has God accomplished through your life?

4. Why did Paul prefer not to minister where others had already ministered? What might be the positives and negatives of such a decision?

5. What principles of evangelism from Paul's life are you seeking to apply in your life?

INSPIRATION

An electrical storm caused a blackout in our neighborhood. When the lights went out, I felt my way through the darkness into the storage closet where we keep the candles for nights like this . . . I took my match and lit four of them . . . I was turning to leave with the large candle in my hand when I heard a voice, "Now, hold it right there."

"Who said that?"

"I did." The voice was near my hand.

"Who are you? What are you?"

"I'm a candle."

I lifted up the candle to take a closer look. You won't believe what I saw. There was a tiny face in the wax . . . a moving, functioning, fleshlike face full of expression and life.

"Don't take me out of here!"

"What?"

"I said, Don't take me out of this room."

"What do you mean? I have to take you out. You're a candle. Your job is to give light. It's dark out there."

"But you can't take me out. I'm not ready," the candle explained with pleading eyes. "I need more preparation."

I couldn't believe my ears. "More preparation?"

"Yeah, I've decided I need to research this job of light-giving so I won't go out and make a bunch of mistakes. You'd be surprised how distorted the glow of an untrained candle can be."

"All right then," I said. "You're not the only candle on the shelf. I'll blow you out and take the others!"

But just as I got my cheeks full of air, I heard other voices.

"We aren't going either!"

I turned around and looked at the three other candles. "You are candles and your job is to light dark places!"

"Well, that may be what you think," said the candle on the far left . . . "You may think we have to go, but I'm busy . . . I'm meditating on the importance of light. It's really enlightening."

"And you other two," I asked, "are you going to stay in here as well?"

A short, fat, purple candle with plump cheeks that reminded me of Santa Claus spoke up. "I'm waiting to get my life together. I'm not stable enough."

The last candle had a female voice, very pleasant to the ear. "I'd like to help," she explained, "but lighting the darkness is not my gift . . . I'm a singer. I sing to other candles to encourage them to burn more brightly." She began a rendition of "This Little Light of Mine." The other three joined in, filling the storage room with singing . . .

I took a step back and considered the absurdity of it all. Four perfectly healthy candles singing to each other about light but refusing to come out of the closet. (From *God Came Near* by Max Lucado)

REACTION

6. How does Paul's example inspire you to get more actively involved in evangelism?

7. What has hindered your witness for Christ? Which of the candles in the above story most closely represents your life?

8. How can you overcome that hindrance?

9. Are you reluctant to talk about God with others? How can you overcome that reluctance?

10. What are some creative ways of sharing the gospel?

11. Who shared the gospel message with you? How can you thank that person, particularly if he or she is no longer available to communicate?

LIFE LESSONS

We end this study of the letter to the Romans with a recurring theme on our minds: How will we treat our neighbors? How will we love those who share our beliefs and those who don't? How will we speak and live out the gospel within the church and to the world? This letter invites us to return to it often for encouragement, direction, and challenge. It drives us to appreciate all that God has done for us. The more we learn to love God, the better we are equipped to love our neighbor.

DEVOTION

Father, forgive us for ignoring the lost; forgive us for selfishly enjoying the gift of your salvation, without sharing it with others; forgive us for the times we have kept our mouths shut, burying the truth of your Word, for fear of ridicule or rejection. Fill us with courage, Father. Use us as instruments of your mercy and grace extended to a world bound by sin.

For more Bible passages on evangelism, see Matthew 5:13–16; 28:18–20; Acts 1:8; 2 Corinthians 2:14–17; 1 Thessalonians 2:8; 1 Peter 3:15–16.

To complete the book of Romans during this twelve-part study, read Romans 15:14–16:27.

JOURNALING

How well is "this little light of mine" shining?

Lucado Life Lesson Series

Revised and updated, the Lucado Life Lessons series is perfect
for small group or individual use and includes intriguing questions
that will take you deeper into God's Word.

THOMAS NELSON
Since 1798

Available at your local Christian Bookstore.

CPSIA information can be obtained at www.ICGtesting.com
Printed in the USA
LVOW06s1955110915

453851LV00018B/162/P